CW00541531

READY, STEADY, PRACTISE!

Rachel Axten-Higgs

Comprehension
Pupil Book Year 4

Features of this book

- Clear explanations and worked examples for each comprehension topic from the KS2 National Curriculum.

- Questions split into three sections that become progressively more challenging:

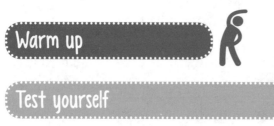

Warm up

Test yourself

Challenge yourself

- 'How did you do?' checks at the end of each topic for self-evaluation.

- Regular progress tests to assess pupils' understanding and recap on their learning.

- Answers to every question in a pull-out section at the centre of the book.

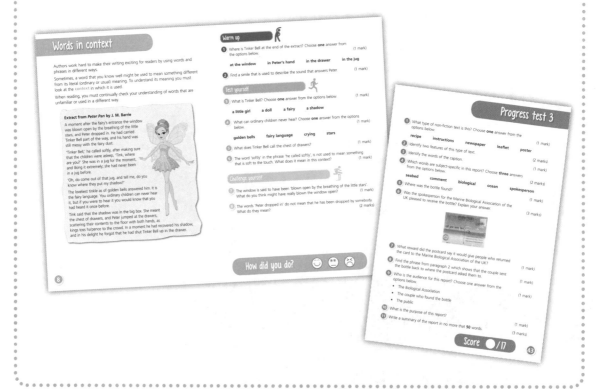

Contents

What are classic stories?

Classic stories are well-known stories that are timeless. They were often written many years ago but are still enjoyed today. For example, because they are so popular, the *Harry Potter* books may withstand the test of time and may become classic stories many years from now.

Classic stories may have old-fashioned language and references to items that are no longer in use today.

Extract from *Swallows and Amazons* by Arthur Ransome

Roger, aged seven, and no longer the youngest of the family, ran in wide zigzags, to and fro, across the steep field that sloped up from the lake to Holly Howe, the farm where they were staying for part of the summer holidays. He ran until he nearly reached the hedge by the footpath, then turned and ran until he nearly reached the hedge on the other side of the field. Then he turned and crossed the field again. Each crossing of the field brought him nearer to the farm. The wind was against him, and he was tacking up against it to the farm, where at the gate his patient mother was awaiting him. He could not run straight against the wind because he was a sailing vessel, a tea-clipper, the *Cutty Sark*. His elder brother John had said only that morning that steamships were just engines in tin boxes. Sail was the thing, and so, though it took rather longer, Roger made his way up the field in broad tacks.

When he came near his mother, he saw that she had in her hand a red envelope and a small piece of white paper, a telegram.

1 Why is this book a classic? Choose **one** option from the list below. (1 mark)

- It was written recently.
- It was written some time ago and is still read today.
- It is a fun story to read.

2 What old-fashioned form of communication is mentioned in the text? (1 mark)

Test yourself

3 How old is Roger? Choose **one** option from the list below. (1 mark)

10   **8**   **7**   **9**

4 What time of year is it? Choose **one** option from the list below. (1 mark)

autumn   **summer**   **winter**   **spring**

5 Write this description, filling in the missing words. (2 marks)

… the steep field that sloped up from the _____ to _____

6 Find and copy the phrase John uses to describe steamships. (1 mark)

Challenge yourself

7 Why was Roger running in a zigzag across the field? (2 marks)

8 Write the title of another classic story. (1 mark)

How did you do?

Themes in classic stories

A **theme** is an idea in a text – an idea the author wants you to think about. The author does not tell you what the theme is. You have to figure it out for yourself from what happens, what the characters do and what they say.

Some themes are found in many books. For example, good and evil, rags to riches, rewards for good deeds.

Extract from *The Wind in the Willows* by Kenneth Grahame

The Badger drew himself up, took a firm grip of his stick with both paws, glanced round at his comrades, and cried:

'The hour is come! Follow me!'

And flung the door open wide.

My!

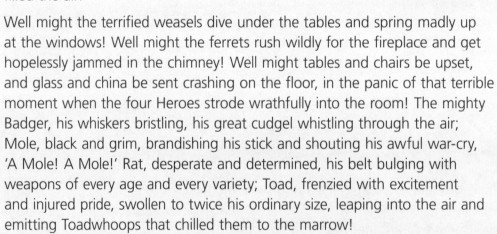

What a squealing and a squeaking and a screeching filled the air!

Well might the terrified weasels dive under the tables and spring madly up at the windows! Well might the ferrets rush wildly for the fireplace and get hopelessly jammed in the chimney! Well might tables and chairs be upset, and glass and china be sent crashing on the floor, in the panic of that terrible moment when the four Heroes strode wrathfully into the room! The mighty Badger, his whiskers bristling, his great cudgel whistling through the air; Mole, black and grim, brandishing his stick and shouting his awful war-cry, 'A Mole! A Mole!' Rat, desperate and determined, his belt bulging with weapons of every age and every variety; Toad, frenzied with excitement and injured pride, swollen to twice his ordinary size, leaping into the air and emitting Toadwhoops that chilled them to the marrow!

…

The affair was soon over. Up and down, the whole length of the hall, strode the four Friends, whacking with their sticks at every head that showed itself; and in five minutes the room was cleared.

1 Who are the four 'Heroes'? (1 mark)

2 What animals were the Heroes fighting? (1 mark)

Test yourself

3 One of the characters is described as 'desperate and determined'.
Choose **one** character from the list below to whom this refers. (1 mark)

Rat **Mole** **Toad** **Badger**

4 What was Badger carrying when he entered? (1 mark)

5 Where does the action take place? Choose **one** option from the list below. (1 mark)

outside **on the river** **in a hall** **in the wild wood**

6 What verb is used to show how the weasels got under the table? (1 mark)

Challenge yourself

7 What is the main theme of this extract? Choose **one** option from the
list below. (1 mark)

rags to riches **good conquers evil** **reward for good deeds**

8 Re-read the information you are given about Toad during the battle.
Write, in your own words (using modern words) what he was doing. (2 marks)

How did you do?

Words in context

Authors work hard to make their writing exciting for readers by using words and phrases in different ways.

Sometimes, a word that you know well might be used to mean something different from its literal (ordinary or usual) meaning. To understand its meaning you must look at the context in which it is used.

When reading, you must continually check your understanding of words that are unfamiliar or used in a different way.

Extract from *Peter Pan* by J. M. Barrie

A moment after the fairy's entrance the window was blown open by the breathing of the little stars, and Peter dropped in. He had carried Tinker Bell part of the way, and his hand was still messy with the fairy dust.

'Tinker Bell,' he called softly, after making sure that the children were asleep, 'Tink, where are you?' She was in a jug for the moment, and liking it extremely; she had never been in a jug before.

'Oh, do come out of that jug, and tell me, do you know where they put my shadow?'

The loveliest tinkle as of golden bells answered him. It is the fairy language. You ordinary children can never hear it, but if you were to hear it you would know that you had heard it once before.

Tink said that the shadow was in the big box. She meant the chest of drawers, and Peter jumped at the drawers, scattering their contents to the floor with both hands, as kings toss ha'pence to the crowd. In a moment he had recovered his shadow, and in his delight he forgot that he had shut Tinker Bell up in the drawer.

1 Where is Tinker Bell at the end of the extract? Choose **one** answer from the options below. (1 mark)

at the window   **in Peter's hand**   **in the drawer**   **in the jug**

2 Find a simile that is used to describe the sound that answers Peter. (1 mark)

Test yourself

3 What is Tinker Bell? Choose **one** answer from the options below. (1 mark)

a little girl   **a doll**   **a fairy**   **a shadow**

4 What can ordinary children never hear? Choose **one** answer from the options below. (1 mark)

golden bells   **fairy language**   **crying**   **stars**

5 What does Tinker Bell call the chest of drawers? (1 mark)

6 The word 'softly' in the phrase 'he called softly', is not used to mean something that is soft to the touch. What does it mean in this context? (1 mark)

Challenge yourself

7 The window is said to have been 'blown open by the breathing of the little stars'. What do you think might have really blown the window open? (1 mark)

8 The words 'Peter dropped in' do not mean that he has been dropped by somebody. What do they mean? (2 marks)

How did you do?

9

The structure of myths

Myths are stories about gods and goddesses. Many have a religious message. Some have a message about what happens because of people's wishes or actions.

Many myths are about amazing events and characters, animals and objects that have magical powers.

The Midas Touch

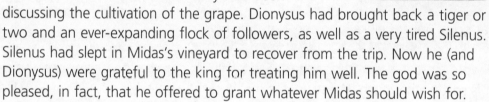

Midas was king of Phrygia. One day his farmhands brought him a creature who was part-man and part-goat. They had found him sleeping in the vineyard and tied him up to stop him escaping. Midas immediately recognised the creature as Silenus, who was the right-hand man to the god Dionysus. He quickly ordered that he be set free.

Silenus explained that he and his master had just returned from the East where they had been discussing the cultivation of the grape. Dionysus had brought back a tiger or two and an ever-expanding flock of followers, as well as a very tired Silenus. Silenus had slept in Midas's vineyard to recover from the trip. Now he (and Dionysus) were grateful to the king for treating him well. The god was so pleased, in fact, that he offered to grant whatever Midas should wish for.

Midas didn't have to think twice; he believed that he would be happy if he could continually restock the gold in his royal treasury, so he asked that everything he touch be turned to gold. Dionysus paused, checked twice whether this is what Midas really wanted, and then waved his sceptre and the wish was granted.

Midas quickly returned home to have a go. He was unsure to begin with and laid a shaking hand on a bowl of fruit and then a stool. Each of these turned to the purest gold.

'Look at this!' he boasted, turning his chariot into solid gold (which made it worthless as it could no longer move). He then took his young daughter by the hand to show her more, forgetting that she would turn to gold – a golden statue.

'Oh no!' cried Midas. As he touched more things he realised that he couldn't touch any useful object without it becoming useless (yet priceless), nor any food, nor any person.

It was at this point that Midas understood why Dionysus had been reluctant to grant the wish and had checked with him twice before granting it.

Fortunately, Dionysus was very kind, and very forgiving. He allowed Midas to wash away his magic touch in the river Pactolus.

1. What is the name of the god in this story? (1 mark)

2. Why was Silenus in Midas' vineyard? Choose **one** answer from the options below. (1 mark)

   • He was hiding from Dionysus.

   • He was spying on Midas.

   • He was sleeping to recover from his trip.

   • He was stealing grapes.

Test yourself

3. Who was the creature sleeping in the vineyard? Choose **one** answer from the options below. (1 mark)

   a goat   **Silenus**   **Dionysus**   **Midas**

4. How many times did Dionysus check with Midas about his wish? Choose **one** answer from the options below. (1 mark)

   once   **three times**   **five times**   **twice**

5. Why was Midas unsure to start with when he had his wish? (2 marks)

6. Why do you think Dionysus let Midas reverse his wish? (2 marks)

Challenge yourself

7. In your own words, what did Midas learn in this myth? (2 marks)

8. Did Dionysus realise that Midas was making a mistake when he made his wish? Explain your answer fully. (2 marks)

How did you do?

Themes of legends

Legends, like myths, tell us about how people lived, what they believed, what they valued and what they were afraid of.

Legends have many of the themes that are used in traditional stories, for example:

- good versus evil / wise versus foolish / strong versus weak / just versus unjust
- magic and the supernatural
- rags to riches / riches to rags
- a quest, a search or a journey.

William Tell

One day, William Tell decided to go to his nearest town with his son, Walter, to collect provisions. When they reached the town they immediately felt uneasy as there were soldiers everywhere. As they walked across the square, Tell noticed a tall pole with an expensive hat perched on top and soldiers guarding it. He thought it very strange to have a hat on a pole! He pulled his son closer and carried on walking.

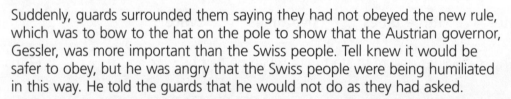

Suddenly, guards surrounded them saying they had not obeyed the new rule, which was to bow to the hat on the pole to show that the Austrian governor, Gessler, was more important than the Swiss people. Tell knew it would be safer to obey, but he was angry that the Swiss people were being humiliated in this way. He told the guards that he would not do as they had asked.

He was immediately arrested and the guards went to fetch the governor, Gessler. When Gessler arrived, he demanded to know why Tell would not bow to the hat. Tell told him he did not want to. Gessler said he was a stupid Swiss man and told the guards to imprison him. Just as Gessler was leaving, Walter called after him and said that his father was not stupid; in fact, he was the best shot with a crossbow in the whole of Switzerland.

Gessler said he would let Tell go if he could hit an apple on the head of Walter at a hundred paces. Tell refused to put his son in danger, but Gessler said that he would kill Walter if he did not accept the challenge. William Tell had no choice.

Tell was nervous, but Walter reassured him. Walter trusted his father completely and showed him he was not afraid. Tell took two bolts from his quiver and fired one. *Thwack*! The apple splintered into hundreds of pieces. The Swiss people cheered. Tell made to leave with his son.

Gessler stopped him to ask what the second bolt was for. Tell told him that, had it gone wrong, he would have used it to shoot him. When Gessler told the guards to arrest Tell and his son, Tell had no choice but to use the bolt to rid the world of Gessler, thus giving the Swiss people their freedom once again.

1 Using the themes in the introduction on page 12, which **two** themes do you think this story reflects? (2 marks)

2 Using evidence from the text, where does the story take place? Choose **one** answer from the options below. (1 mark)

England   **Austria**   **Switzerland**   **Germany**

Test yourself

3 What was the name of the governor? Choose **one** answer from the options below. (1 mark)

William Tell   **Walter Tell**   **Gessler**   **Emperor**

4 When Walter and William first arrived in the town, what made them uneasy? (1 mark)

5 Would you have bowed to the hat? Explain your answer. (1 mark)

6 Which sentence in the text shows that Tell hit the apple from Walter's head? (1 mark)

Challenge yourself

7 Do you think it was right for William Tell to kill the governor? Explain your answer. (2 marks)

8 What does 'giving the Swiss people their freedom once again' mean? (2 marks)

How did you do?

Complex characters

Some **characters** are good role models, showing us how we should behave, for example Superman or Little Red Riding Hood.

Some characters show us how not to behave, for example the Big Bad Wolf or Voldemort.

Like people in real life, though, characters can be bad in one moment but good in the next. Like us, they do not always understand why they do things and they can be quite **complex**.

Extract from *The Lion, the Witch and the Wardrobe* by C. S. Lewis

You mustn't think that even now Edmund was quite so bad that he actually wanted his brother and sisters to be turned into stone. He did want Turkish Delight and to be a Prince (and later a King) and to pay Peter out for calling him a beast. As for what the Witch would do with the others, he didn't want her to be particularly nice to them – certainly not to put them on the same level as himself; but he managed to believe, or to pretend he believed, that she wouldn't do anything very bad to them, 'Because,' he said to himself, 'all these people who say nasty things about her are her enemies and probably half of it isn't true. She was jolly nice to me, anyway, much nicer than they are. I expect she is the rightful Queen really. Anyway, she'll be better than that awful Aslan!' At least, that was the excuse he made in his own mind for what he was doing. It wasn't a very good excuse, however, for deep down inside him he really knew that the White Witch was bad and cruel.

1 Name **two** things that Edmund wants that the White Witch could give him. (1 mark)

2 Give **two** more examples of good characters from stories you have read. (1 mark)

Test yourself

3 What is the name of Edmund's brother? Choose **one** answer from the options below. (1 mark)

Peter   **White Witch**   **Edmund**   **Aslan**

4 Did Edmund want his brother and sisters turned to stone? Explain your answer. (2 marks)

5 Find in the text the **two** adjectives that describe what Edmund truly knew about the White Witch. (1 mark)

Challenge yourself

6 Do you think Edmund, from this extract, is a good character, a bad one, or is he a complex character? Why? (2 marks)

7 Did Edmund truly believe the excuse that he made up? Explain how you know. (2 marks)

How did you do?

Arachne the Spinner

Arachne was a young woman who lived in Athens. She had a great talent; she was able to spin beautiful fine thread and weave wonderful cloth. Arachne was well known and very much admired by her fellow Athenians. However, as time passed she grew so proud of her own talents, that she began boasting. She could often be heard saying 'I am the greatest spinner, not only in Athens, but in the whole world!'

Her friends became used to this boasting but always replied by saying, 'Yes you are Arachne, but the goddess Athena still remains the greatest of all spinners!'

To begin with, Arachne accepted these answers, not believing them but not challenging them either. As time passed, however, Arachne became evermore conceited and truly believed that she was better even that the goddess Athena.

One day in the market square, Arachne was boasting as always and was heard to say, 'Athena? She can't spin thread as fine or weave cloth as beautifully as I can. I believe I could even teach her things she does not know!'

An old woman spoke quietly to Arachne warning her never to speak ill of the gods and to only ever treat them with respect. Arachne did not heed this warning, merely laughing and saying, 'Let her come and see me, I'll show her who is the better weaver!'

In a flash, the woman's cloak disappeared and Athena stood before Arachne. She told Arachne that they would have a competition and that whoever won by doing the best weaving, the loser must never weave again. Arachne, believing in her own abilities, agreed to this plan.

Arachne wove beautiful light, fine cloth that looked like silken web. The people watching were amazed at its radiance. Athena then finished at her loom and held up her work. She had woven flowers, a stream, clouds, blue sky and the gods themselves into her cloth. It was truly incredible. The people of Athens were filled with wonder at what they saw; even Arachne had no choice but to admit that she had lost the contest.

Athena could not bear to see Arachne crying at the prospect of never being able to weave again. She could not, however, break the agreement they made. Instead she turned Arachne into a spider so that she could continue to spin and weave.

This is why some people say that all spiders in the world are the children of Arachne.

1 What type of story is this? Choose **one** answer from the options below.   (1 mark)

classic story   myth   legend   fairy tale

2 Explain your answer to question 1, using your knowledge of story types.   (1 mark)

3 What **two** important lessons did Arachne learn?   (2 marks)

4 Explain what is meant by 'not challenging them either'? Choose **one** answer from the options below.   (1 mark)

- She didn't fight with Athena.
- She didn't fight with her friends.
- She didn't disagree with what her friends were saying.
- She knew that she was wrong so didn't say anything.

5 Find and write the word that is used to mean the same as **competition**.   (1 mark)

6 Explain what the word **conceited** means, using the context of the story to help you.   (1 mark)

7 It says that 'Arachne wove beautiful light, fine cloth …' Explain which meaning of the word **light** is meant here.   (1 mark)

8 Do you think Arachne was a bad character? Explain your answer.   (2 marks)

9 Did Arachne lose the competition because she could not weave? Explain your answer.   (2 marks)

10 Find and write the phrase that is used to show that Arachne believed she would win the competition.   (1 mark)

Score ⬤ / 13   17

Characterisation

It is the author's job to let us know the personality of the character and this is called characterisation.

Characters need to be life-like and this is achieved by describing their behaviour and the decisions they make, what they say and how they say it.

At times, an author may choose to reveal the thoughts that run through a character's mind.

Extract from *The Railway Children* by Edith Nesbit

The Station Master loosened Peter's collar, struck a match and looked at them by its flickering light.

'Why,' said he, 'you're the children from the Three Chimneys up yonder. So nicely dressed, too. Tell me now, what made you do such a thing? Haven't you been to church? …' He spoke much more gently now, and Peter said:–

'I didn't think it was stealing. I was almost sure it wasn't. I thought if I took it from the outside part of the heap, perhaps it would be. But in the middle I thought I could fairly count it only mining. It'll take thousands of years for you to burn up all that coal and get to the middle parts.'

'Not quite. But did you do it for a lark* or what?'

'Not much lark carting that beastly heavy stuff up the hill,' said Peter, indignantly.

'Then why did you?' The Station Master's voice was so much kinder now that Peter replied:

'You know that wet day? Well, Mother said we were too poor to have a fire. We always had fires when it was cold at our other house, and –'

'DON'T!' interrupted Bobbie, in a whisper.

'Well,' said the Station Master, rubbing his chin thoughtfully, 'I'll tell you what I'll do. I'll look over it this once …'

*A **lark** is a harmless joke or a bit of fun.

1 Why did Peter take the coal? (1 mark)

2 Why do you think the Station Master let Peter off this time? (1 mark)

Test yourself

3 What did Peter think he was doing in the middle of the coal pile? Choose **one** answer from the options below. (1 mark)

stealing   **borrowing**   **mining**   **digging**

4 How does Bobbie feel when she says 'DON'T!'. Choose **two** answers from the options below. (1 mark)

happy   **embarrassed**   **sad**   **angry**

5 Where did the light come from that allowed the Station Master to see Peter? (1 mark)

6 What is the name of the house where the children live? (1 mark)

Challenge yourself

7 Do you think Peter is a bad character? Explain your answer, using evidence from the text. (1 mark)

8 Do you think that what Peter did was stealing? Explain your answer. (2 marks)

Drawing inferences

Here is an example of how authors tell you more than they say directly:

Freya looked at her watch, grabbed her bag and ran to the school bus stop. When she got there, she realised that she had forgotten her lunchbox. Instead of going back for it, she got on the bus.

We know that Freya catches the bus to school, can read the time on a watch, took her bag with her and forgot her lunch because the author says so directly. We can infer that she is running late, that she only just got to the bus stop on time (as she could not go back for her lunch) and that she will need to find lunch at school or go without.

The Lion and the Mouse

A lion, who was king of the jungle, was bored and fed up. He watched a mouse collecting food for its family before he trapped its tail under his enormous paw.

'Please don't eat me!' squeaked the mouse. 'My family needs this food. I promise to help you one day when you are most in need.'

The lion laughed. 'How will you ever be able to help me? But, you are a brave little mouse so I will let you go.'

A few days later, hunters managed to catch the lion in a big, strong net. The lion was angry and roared so that the whole jungle could hear him. He wriggled about, trying to free himself but only managed to get himself more tangled. Despite his strength, he could not break the net.

Suddenly, the little mouse appeared. Without hesitation, he chewed through the net and the lion was soon free.

'Thank you, my friend,' said the lion. 'I did not believe you when you said that you would be able to help me one day, but now I do! I freed you and now you have set me free!'

1 Which words show that the mouse immediately started to free the lion?   (1 mark)

2 Why does the lion describe the mouse as 'brave' at the beginning?   (1 mark)

Test yourself

3 How did the lion set the mouse free? Choose **one** answer from the options below.   (1 mark)

- He stopped the monkeys from hurting him.
- He helped the mouse to chew through the net.
- He let him go instead of eating him.

4 Why did the lion laugh and question how the mouse could ever help him?   (2 marks)

5 What did the lion learn about the mouse in the story?   (1 mark)

Challenge yourself

6 Identify **two** things that the author has told you about the mouse.   (2 marks)

7 How did the mouse know that the lion had been caught?   (1 mark)

8 Why did the lion think that the mouse would never be able to help him?   (1 mark)

Justifying inferences

Justifying inferences is an important skill. You need to first draw a conclusion or make a judgement about something that you are told by an author. You must then scan the text further, to identify evidence that supports inference. If you cannot find any evidence, you might need to rethink your inference.

Extract from *The Wonderful Wizard of Oz* by L. Frank Baum

Just as he spoke there came from the forest a terrible roar, and the next moment a great Lion bounded into the road. With one blow of his paw he sent the Scarecrow spinning over and over to the edge of the road, and then he struck at the Tin Woodman with his sharp claws. But, to the Lion's surprise, he could make no impression on the tin, although the Woodman fell over in the road and lay still.

Little Toto, now that he had an enemy to face, ran barking toward the Lion, and the great beast had opened his mouth to bite the dog, when Dorothy, fearing Toto would be killed, and heedless of danger, rushed forward and slapped the Lion upon his nose as hard as she could, while she cried out:

'Don't you dare to bite Toto! You ought to be ashamed of yourself, a big beast like you, to bite a poor little dog!'

'I didn't bite him,' said the Lion, as he rubbed his nose with his paw where Dorothy had hit it.

'No, but you tried to,' she retorted. 'You are nothing but a big coward.'

'I know it,' said the Lion, hanging his head in shame. 'I've always known it. But how can I help it?'

'I don't know, I'm sure. To think of your striking a stuffed man, like the poor Scarecrow!'

Answers

Pages 4–5
1. It was written some time ago and is still read today (**1 mark**)
2. telegram (**1 mark**)
3. 7 (**1 mark**)
4. summer (**1 mark**)
5. … the steep field that sloped up from the **lake**, to **Holly Howe** (**1 mark** for each word)
6. 'just engines in tin boxes' (**1 mark** for direct quote from text)
7. He was pretending to be a sailboat tacking against the wind. (**2 marks** for he was being a sailboat tacking against the wind; **1 mark** for an answer that states that he was a boat but does not mention the wind)
8. Check children are writing titles of classic stories, e.g. *Wind in the Willows, Just so Stories, The Railway Children* (**1 mark**)

Pages 6–7
1. Badger, Mole, Rat and Toad (**1 mark**)
2. ferrets and weasels (**1 mark**)
3. Rat (**1 mark**)
4. a stick/cudgel (**1 mark**)
5. in a hall (**1 mark**)
6. dive (**1 mark**)
7. good conquers evil (**1 mark**)
8. Toad was excited but also had lost his pride/he had grown in size/he was jumping/he was making loud noises that scared the others (**2 marks** for three or four; **1 mark** for two)

Pages 8–9
1. in the drawer (**1 mark**)
2. as of golden bells (**1 mark**)
3. a fairy (**1 mark**)
4. fairy language (**1 mark**)
5. 'the big box' (**1 mark** for this direct quote from text)
6. quietly/gently (**1 mark**)
7. the wind outside (**1 mark**)
8. That he has come through the window and landed on the floor as if from nowhere (as if he has been dropped from the sky) (**2 marks** for answering he has come through the window and a link to appearing from nowhere; **1 mark** for an answer that identifies he has come through the window but does not link to the word *dropped*)

Pages 10–11
1. Dionysus (**1 mark**)
2. he was sleeping to recover from his trip (**1 mark**)
3. Silenus (**1 mark**)
4. twice (**1 mark**)
5. He had been given a new skill and he didn't know if it would work (**2 marks** for linking the new skill with the not knowing if it would work; **1 mark** for stating that it was a new skill **or** he did not know if it would work)
6. Dionysus knew that Midas had learned his lesson and that he would not be greedy again (**1 mark**); he also knew that he could not carry on living in that way (**1 mark**)
7. Midas learned not to be greedy (**1 mark**); although things can be worth a lot of money when they are gold, some things are better as they are (**1 mark**)
8. Yes (**1 mark**); he paused and checked twice which shows that he knew it would not be a good idea (**1 mark**)

Pages 12–13
1. Any two from the following: good vs evil; just vs unjust; strong vs weak; wise vs foolish (**2 marks** for two correct; **1 mark** for one)
2. Switzerland (**1 mark**)
3. Gessler (**1 mark**)
4. the number of soldiers (**1 mark**)
5. **Yes**, because it would have meant that I was safe. **No**, because Gessler was a bully. (**1 mark** for choosing an answer and writing a plausible explanation that matches chosen answer)
6. The apple splintered into hundreds of pieces (**1 mark**)
7. **Yes**, I think it was right because the governor had gone back on his promise to let William Tell's son go and he was mean to the local people. He would probably have killed William Tell anyway. OR **No**, I think he should not have killed the governor because you should never kill people. You should find another way to sort things out (**2 marks** for answer that contains a judgment and two pieces of evidence; **1 mark** for answer with a judgment and one piece of evidence)
8. Gessler was killed by William Tell with the second bolt (**1 mark**) because he ordered the guards to arrest him and his son (**1 mark**)

Pages 14–15
1. Any two of: Turkish Delight; to be a Prince; to be a King; to pay Peter back for being mean (**1 mark**)
2. Any two characters that are 'good' characters from well-known stories (**1 mark** for two correct names)
3. Peter (**1 mark**)
4. No, because it says that he didn't in the first sentence of text (**1 mark** for writing No; **1 mark** for an explanation that states that the answer is in the text)
5. bad, cruel (**1 mark** for both correct)

Answers

6. **Good**, because he did not really want his brother and sisters harmed. **Bad**, because he wants to betray his brother and sisters and find the White Witch, even though he knows she is bad. (Either answer acceptable; **2 marks** for one that is backed up with two pieces of evidence from the text; **1 mark** for only one piece of evidence)

7. No, because at the end it says that deep down he knew that the Witch was cruel (**1 mark** for writing No; **1 mark** for an explanation that uses evidence from the text)

Pages 16–17

1. myth (**1 mark**)
2. It is about gods and goddesses (**1 mark**)
3. Not to underestimate the gods and goddesses/not to boast (**1 mark** for each)
4. She didn't disagree with what her friends were saying (**1 mark**)
5. contest (**1 mark**)
6. proud/sure of oneself or vain (**1 mark**)
7. e.g. not heavy (**1 mark**)
8. No (**1 mark**); she just became too big headed, she was foolish, she made mistakes (**1 mark** for any plausible reason)
9. No (**1 mark**); she could weave beautiful cloth: 'the people were amazed by its radiance' but Athena could weave even better cloth (**1 mark**)
10. believing in her own abilities (**1 mark**)

Pages 18–19

1. He wanted to be able to provide coal for the family, even though they were poor (**1 mark**)
2. He felt sorry for them when Peter explained why he had done it (**1 mark**)
3. mining (**1 mark**)
4. embarrassed, sad (**1 mark** for both)
5. a lit match (**1 mark**)
6. The Three Chimneys (**1 mark**)
7. **No**, because he took the coal to look after his family. **Yes**, because it is wrong to steal (**1 mark** for choosing an answer and writing a plausible explanation that matches the answer)
8. Yes (**1 mark**), because he took something that did not belong to him without permission (**1 mark**)

Pages 20–21

1. Without hesitation (**1 mark**)
2. He has stood up to the lion rather than staying silent when he was caught (**1 mark**)
3. He let him go instead of eating him (**1 mark**)
4. The lion laughed because the mouse was so small (**1 mark**); He is so big and did not believe that he would ever need help from a mouse (**1 mark**)
5. That even though he was small, he could be helpful to the lion (**1 mark**)

6. Any two things in the story: e.g. the mouse was collecting food for his family; the mouse is brave (**1 mark** for each correct answer)
7. The mouse heard the lion roar (**1 mark**)
8. Because he was so small (**1 mark**)

Pages 22–23

1. barks (**1 mark**)
2. he hangs his head in shame (**1 mark**)
3. a terrible roar (**1 mark**)
4. Dorothy (**1 mark**)
5. 2 (**1 mark**)
6. A person who lacks the courage to do the right thing or endure dangerous or unpleasant things (**1 mark** for a correct explanation – this may be from a dictionary)
7. 'a poor little dog' (**1 mark** for this direct quotation)
8. He is big and strong and he is trying to hurt helpless people and a little dog (**1 mark**)
9. He is stuffed with straw and therefore light, not like a human (**1 mark**)

Pages 24–25

1. At the end of the fifth and sixth lines the poet has used **rhyming words**. Within these lines she has used **repetition** (**1 mark** for both words)
2. weird, woman, woods (**1 mark** for all three)
3. bugs (**1 mark**)
4. thinner (**1 mark**)
5. creaky and squeaky (**1 mark**)
6. roof and stairs (**1 mark** for both)
7. Individual answers based on child's own opinions (**2 marks** for an answer that gives a plausible reason for either Yes or No, and that refers to the actual text; **1 mark** for a reason that is based purely on personal preference, without reference to the actual text)
8. Witch from Hansel and Gretel/A witch (**1 mark**); she lives in a gingerbread house, she cooks children into soup, strange clothes (**1 mark** for two or more reasons)

Pages 26–27

1. 500 years (**1 mark**)
2. River Weser (**1 mark**)
3. rats (**1 mark**)
4. made nests in them (**1 mark**)
5. By making lots of noise so they couldn't hear each other (**1 mark**)
6. Hanover (**1 mark**)
7. cradles (**1 mark**)
8. The beginning (**1 mark**); it is setting the scene for the story (**1 mark**)
9. cheese, soup, sprats (small fish) (**1 mark** for all three)

Pages 28–29

1. Learn to read and write (**1 mark**)
2. copy from another child (**1 mark**)
3. to be able to stay in bed (**1 mark**)
4. second helpings (**1 mark**)
5. She does not want to hear about the naughty things the child has done (**1 mark**)
6. Examples: They learned to read and write/to do something difficult in maths/to play a new game (**1 mark** for each plausible answer, up to a maximum of **2 marks**)
7. An acrostic (**1 mark**); because the first letters of each line spell SCHOOL (**1 mark**)
8. A list poem (**1 mark**); because it is a list of things that the child learned at school (**1 mark**)

Pages 30–31

1. narrative (**1 mark**); it tells a story (**1 mark**)
2. honey and money (**1 mark** for both)
3. delayed (**1 mark**)
4. A year and a day (**1 mark**)
5. repetition and rhyming (**1 mark**)
6. fruit (**1 mark**); **1 mark** for explanation
7. runcible (**1 mark**)
8. vicar (**1 mark**)
9. The Owl and the Pussy-cat set sail/The Owl tells the Pussy-cat that he loves her/They buy a ring from the Pig/They get married/They dance by the light of the moon (**2 marks** for all correct, **1 mark** for three correct)
10. yes (**1 mark**); he sold them the ring for not much money (**1 mark**)

Pages 32–33

1. Dorset (**1 mark**)
2.
   • Deep Sea Adventure
   • Sharky's
   • Brewers Quay
   • Nothe Fort Museum of Coastal Defence
   • Sea Life Park (**3 marks** for all correct; **2 marks** for three or four correct; **1 mark** for two correct)
3. Nothe Fort Museum (**1 mark**)
4. Christmas (**1 mark**)
5. amazing (**1 mark**)
6. Example answer: Nothe Fort Museum, because I would like to learn about maritime history (**3 marks** for answer that is backed up with information given about the place in the guide)
7. relating to the sea (**1 mark**)
8. Children's paragraphs should inform as well as intrigue their reader – they need to make the place sound appealing (**2 marks** for a complete answer which clearly writes for an audience; **1 mark** for simple details given)

Pages 34–35

1. Example answers: **species**: a group of living things that have similar characteristics; **southern hemisphere**: the half of the Earth that is south of the equator; **krill**: shrimp-like animals that live in the open sea; **crustaceans**: animals that usually have a hard covering or exoskeleton, and two pairs of antennae or feelers, e.g. crabs (**1 mark** for each correct definition – check pupils are using dictionaries correctly; max **4 marks**)
2. Africa; New Zealand (**1 mark** for both)
3. Example answer: Penguins' diet; how penguins eat and drink (**1 mark** for a suitable heading that recognises the paragraph is about what penguins eat)
4. They cannot count every penguin in the world (**2 marks** for an explanation that shows that every penguin cannot be counted; **1 mark** for an answer that says it is just a guess, without explanation)
5. shape of their bodies (**1 mark**)
6. It is fresh water rather than salt water (**1 mark**)
7. Check that children have written facts not opinions (**2 marks** for three facts; **1 mark** for two)

Pages 36–37

1. Example answers: Paragraph 1: The Solar System; Paragraph 2: The Sun; Paragraph 3: Mercury (**2 marks** for all correct; **1 mark** for two correct)
2. seven (**1 mark**)
3. 350°C (**1 mark**)
4. elliptical (**1 mark**)
5. 88 (**1 mark**)
6. Any fact that is about the Sun, taken from the article (**1 mark**)
7. explanation (**1 mark**); it gives information about the planets of the solar system, it informs the reader (**1 mark**)
8. e.g. My Very Elderly Mother Just Sat Under Newspaper! (**1 mark** for a plausible mnemonic)

Pages 38–39

1. A recipe or instruction text; the title, ingredients list and numbered steps show its text type (**1 mark** for both)
2. So that you can identify them quickly and easily when making a shopping list or deciding if you are going to enjoy eating it (**1 mark**)
3. 250 (**1 mark**)
4. cool it (**1 mark**)
5. 4 (**1 mark**)
6. put/bring/stir/remove/cool/tip/make/strain/take/serve (**1 mark** for one verb written correctly)

Answers

7. Example answer: Yes, because I like strawberries and blackberries (**2 marks** for an answer using the text; **1 mark** for a plausible answer that does not use the text)
8. Whilst (**1 mark**)
9. blackberry pips (**1 mark**)

Pages 40–41
1. Harry during his record attempt (**1 mark**)
2. Who? Harry Jones; What? Balancing doughnuts on his head; Where? Barnstaple; When? this week; Why? To set a world record (**2 marks** for all correct; **1 mark** for three or four)
3. 44 (**1 mark**)
4. Jones (**1 mark**)
5. Example answer: A Balancing Act (**1 mark** for a plausible headline that is linked to the content of the article – it does not have to be funny)
6. Example answers: **Yes**, it would be good to break Harry's record. Harry practised and persevered and I would want to do this too. **No**, I don't think I could balance more than 44 doughnuts, but I could try balancing something else instead and set a different world record (**2 marks** for a plausible explanation based on evidence from the text; **1 mark** for giving a reason that is not based on details from the article)
7. No (**1 mark**); he did not go to the park and spend time with other people because he was practising for his record (**1 mark**)
8. e.g. 'I am proud of Harry.'/'I am proud to have helped Harry to achieve this record.' (**1 mark**)

Pages 42–43
1. newspaper (**1 mark**)
2. Any two from: columns/headline/caption/ photograph/reporter/quotes from people involved/5 Ws in first paragraph (**1 mark** for each; max. **2 marks**)
3. The well-travelled bottle (**1 mark**)
4. seabed/biological/ocean (**2 marks** for all correct; **1 mark** for two correct and not more than one wrong)
5. Amrum (**1 mark**)
6. Yes (**1 mark**); he says it is 'truly astonishing/ hopeful it is a world record/sent a reward to the couple (**2 marks** for two reasons; **1 mark** for one)
7. an old shilling (**1 mark**)
8. The couple complied with the wishes (of the writer) (**1 mark**)
9. The public (**1 mark**)
10. To tell people about the bottle being found (**1 mark**)
11. Check that children are only including key details to explain the key facts; summaries should be no more than 50 words (max. **3 marks**)

1 We are told that Toto is a dog but what does he **do** that shows the reader that he is one? Choose **one** answer from the options below.   (1 mark)

   runs   barks   strikes   shouts

2 How do you know, from the Lion's actions, that he feels bad about being a 'big coward'.   (1 mark)

Test yourself

3 What did they hear before they saw the Lion? Choose **one** answer from the options below.   (1 mark)

   a horrible roar   **a terrible roar**   **a terrifying roar**   **a loud roar**

4 Who slapped the Lion on the nose? Choose **one** answer from the options below.   (1 mark)

   Tin Woodman   **Scarecrow**   **Toto**   **Dorothy**

5 How many characters in this extract are actually struck by the Lion?   (1 mark)

6 What is a coward?   (1 mark)

7 What phrase does Dorothy use to describe Toto?   (1 mark)

Challenge yourself

8 Why does Dorothy think (**infer**) that the Lion is a 'big coward'?   (1 mark)

9 Why did the Scarecrow fall over so easily?   (1 mark)

How did you do?

Words and phrases in poems

Poets frequently use words and phrases that can be intense and striking, both in terms of their sound and the images they create.

Phrases are often created to fit a **rhythm** or a **rhyme pattern**, and poets sometimes make use of the techniques of repetition (for example, tiger, tiger!), alliteration (for example, creeping cat), simile (for example, he is like a star) and metaphor (for example, he is a star).

Weird is the Woman

Weird is the woman who lives in the woods
and weird are the clothes she wears.
Crooked the roof of her gingerbread house
and crooked the rickety stairs.
Tattered and patched are the curtains that hide
the tattered and patched things decaying inside.

Sneaky and cheeky the children who spy,
leaving their safe little homes nearby.
Creaky and squeaky footsteps on the floor,
creaky and squeaky the hinge on the door.
No time to run from what stands there …
a tiny old lady with bugs in her hair.

'Come in my dears, I'm about to have dinner.
I'll disappear if I get any thinner!
I look forward to children coming to snoop,
it gives me something to put in my soup!'

1 Complete the sentences by using **two** words from the box below.   (1 mark)

> alliteration   rhyming words   repetition   capital letters

At the end of the fifth and sixth lines the poet has used _____.

Within these lines she has used _____.

2 Which **three** words in the first line make use of alliteration?   (1 mark)

3 What did the lady have in her hair? Choose **one** answer from the
options below.   (1 mark)

cobwebs   food   bugs   clips

4 Which word has been used to rhyme with **dinner**?   (1 mark)

5 Which **two** adjectives are repeated in stanza two?   (1 mark)

6 In the house, what **two** things are crooked?   (1 mark)

7 Do you like the poem? Explain your answer.   (2 marks)

8 Which fairy tale character is this poem written about? Explain your answer
fully using the text.   (2 marks)

How did you do?

Narrative poetry

Narrative poems are the oldest form of poetry. They tell stories with a beginning (which introduces the background to the story), a middle (which relates the main events) and an end (which concludes and summarises the story). In times when most people did not read or write, people shared stories verbally and in a style that was almost song-like. Indeed, songs that you hear nowadays are simply poems that have been set to music.

Extract from 'The Pied Piper of Hamelin' by Robert Browning

Hamelin Town's in Brunswick,

By famous Hanover city;

The river Weser, deep and wide,

Washes its walls on either side;

A pleasanter spot you never spied;

But, when begins my ditty*,

Almost five hundred years ago,

To see the townsfolk suffer so

From vermin*, was a pity.

Rats!

They fought the dogs and killed the cats,

And bit the babies in the cradles,

And ate the cheeses out of the vats*,

And licked the soup from the cooks' own ladles,

Split open the kegs of salted sprats*.

Made nests inside men's Sunday hats.

And even spoiled the women's chats

By drowning their speaking

With shrieking and squeaking

In fifty different sharps and flats.

*__ditty__: a song or poem; __vermin__: nuisance animals;
__vats__: containers; __sprats__: small fish

1 The author refers to events in the poem that happened how many years ago? Choose **one** answer from the options below. (1 mark)

600 years   500 years   200 years   100 years

2 What is the name of the river in the town of Brunswick? (1 mark)

Test yourself

3 What does the word 'vermin' refer to in this poem? Choose **one** answer from the options below. (1 mark)

pipers   children   adults   rats

4 What did the rats do to the men's hats? Choose **one** answer from the options below. (1 mark)

split them open   licked soup from them
made nests in them   ate them

5 How did the rats spoil the women's chats? (1 mark)

6 Which city is Brunswick near to? (1 mark)

7 Which word has been used to rhyme with 'ladles'? (1 mark)

Challenge yourself

8 Is this extract taken from the beginning, the middle or end of the poem? How do you know? (2 marks)

9 Find in this extract **three** foods that the rats ate. (1 mark)

How did you do?

Forms of poetry

Poetry comes in many different **forms**: rhyming poems, narrative poems, acrostic poems, list poems, shape poems, number poems, to mention but a few.

It is important to be able to recognise some of these poems, not just by content, but by form. For example, a list poem contains a list of things, an acrostic poem spells a word with the first letter of each line, and a narrative poem tells a story.

'School'

Starting early;

Cornflakes eaten.

How I wish I could stay in bed!

Once there, I learn to read and write;

Only then will I achieve success.

Learning is so rewarding!

'Learning'

The other day, my mother asked me what
I had learned at school,

I scratched my head and said:

'How to read a book upside down.

How to get second helpings of lunch.

How to talk to my friend without the teacher noticing.

How to copy maths sums from another book.

How to draw funny faces on the bottom of the table.

How to chew gum without being caught.

And, how to wriggle out of trouble.'

It is funny that every day this week …

she has not asked me that question again!

Warm up

1 How will the child in 'School' achieve success? (1 mark)

2 What does the child in 'Learning' do in maths that does not help him to learn? (1 mark)

Test yourself

3 What does the child wish for in 'School'? Choose **one** answer from the options below. (1 mark)

- To be able to read and write.
- To be able to have toast.
- To be able to stay in bed.

4 What did the child in 'Learning' learn to get at lunchtime? Choose **one** answer from the options below. (1 mark)

second helpings   **detention**   **a newspaper**   **a football**

5 Why might the mother in 'Learning' not have asked the same question again? (1 mark)

6 What might the mother have expected the child to have learned at school? (2 marks)

Challenge yourself

7 What form of poem is 'School'? How do you know? (2 marks)

8 What form of poem is 'Learning'? How do you know? (2 marks)

How did you do?

'The Owl and the Pussy-cat' by Edward Lear

I

The Owl and the Pussy-cat went to sea
  In a beautiful pea-green boat,
They took some honey, and plenty of money,
  Wrapped up in a five pound note.
The Owl looked up to the stars above,
  And sang to a small guitar,
'O lovely Pussy! O Pussy my love,
   What a beautiful Pussy you are,
     You are,
     You are!
What a beautiful Pussy you are!'

II

Pussy said to the Owl, 'You elegant fowl!
  How charmingly sweet you sing!
O let us be married! too long we have tarried:
  But what shall we do for a ring?'
They sailed away, for a year and a day,
  To the land where the Bong-tree grows
And there in a wood a Piggy-wig stood
  With a ring at the end of his nose,
     His nose,
     His nose,
With a ring at the end of his nose.

III

'Dear pig, are you willing to sell for one shilling
  Your ring?' Said the Piggy, 'I will.'
So they took it away, and were married next day
  By the Turkey who lives on the hill.
They dined on mince, and slices of quince,
  Which they ate with a runcible spoon;
And hand in hand, on the edge of the sand,
  They danced by the light of the moon,
     The moon,
     The moon,
They danced by the light of the moon.

1 What type of poem is this? Choose **one** answer from the options below. Explain your answer. (2 marks)

    acrostic   **narrative**   **list**   **shape**

2 What did the Owl and the Pussy-cat take with them in the boat? (1 mark)

3 Using the context of the poem, what does 'tarried' mean? Choose **one** answer from the options below. (1 mark)

    delayed   **danced**   **cried**   **sailed**

4 How long did it take them to get to the land where the Pig lived? (1 mark)

5 What features of poetry are used in this poem? Choose **two** answers from the options below. (1 mark)

    repetition   **simile**   **metaphor**   **rhyming**

6 What type of food is a quince? Choose **one** answer from the options below. Explain your answer. (2 marks)

    meat   **fruit**   **pasta**   **biscuit**

7 Edward Lear, the poet who wrote this poem, used nonsense words (words with no real meaning) in some of his poetry. Find the nonsense word used in **stanza III** of the poem. (1 mark)

8 If the Turkey were a human, what job would he have, based on what he does in the poem? (1 mark)

9 Copy the following statements in the order in which they happen in the poem. (2 marks)

- The Owl tells the Pussy-cat that he loves her.
- They get married.
- The Owl and the Pussy-cat set sail.
- They dance by the light of the moon.
- They buy a ring from the Pig.

10 Was the Pig a kind character? Explain your answer. (2 marks)

Score ⬤ / 14

Summarising ideas

A useful skill for reading is being able to scan longer texts and write notes or bullet points about **key information**.

This skill can make things clearer in your mind and can help in practical ways in everyday life. For example, a tourist guide book might give many ideas about things to do on holiday, so writing your own short notes as you read could help you to decide what to do.

A Visitor's Guide to Weymouth, Dorset

The seaside town of Weymouth, in the county of Dorset, is a gateway to the Jurassic Coast. It was originally a fishing village and played a key role in the D-Day invasion.

The Esplanade looks over Weymouth Bay, which is a safe beach with golden sand. The water is clear and shallow so provides the opportunity for safe bathing. The seafront has a wide variety of restaurants, pubs, cafes and small shops.

Even if it is raining, you will never be bored in Weymouth because there are so many interesting places to visit.

The Deep Sea Adventure has a Titanic Exhibition, whilst Sharky's is an indoor children's play zone full of exciting opportunities.

Brewers Quay houses the Timewalk attraction, which explores Weymouth's past, whilst the Nothe Fort Museum of Coastal Defence gives visitors a memorable insight into Weymouth's maritime history.

The Sea Life Park has lots of marine creatures, from seals to sharks and even turtles!

There are also lots of amazing events held in Weymouth throughout the year, including an international kite festival, military parades, volleyball and sailing championships, a carnival in August and a Christmas Day swim in the harbour!

If all that isn't enough, Weymouth even has the best sunshine record in England, even in winter!

1 In which county is Weymouth? (1 mark)

2 Write a bullet point list of the places in Weymouth mentioned in the fourth, fifth and sixth paragraphs. (3 marks)

Test yourself

3 Where can you learn about Weymouth's maritime history? Choose **one** answer from the options below. (1 mark)

Nothe Fort Museum   **Sea Life Park**   **Brewers Quay**

4 When is there a special swim in the harbour? Choose **one** answer from the options below. (1 mark)

Easter   **Christmas**   **August**   **Summer**

5 What adjective is used to describe the events in Weymouth? (1 mark)

6 If your family were going to Weymouth, write down **three** places you would like to visit and why (based on information given in the guide). (3 marks)

Challenge yourself

7 From the text, what do you think the word 'marine' means? (1 mark)

8 Write a paragraph about the village, town or city where you live. Try to make it sound appealing to your reader. (2 marks)

How did you do?

Language of non-fiction texts

All non-fiction text will have some form of subject-specific vocabulary. For example, text about the Internet will have ICT-specific language, such as *computer, Internet, modem.*

By reading non-fiction texts, you will develop your vocabulary because of these subject-specific words.

Penguins

Penguins are birds that cannot fly. The name 'penguin' comes from the Welsh words *pen,* meaning 'head', and *gwyn,* meaning 'white' – 'white head'!

There are 17 species of penguin, which are all slightly different from each other. All of the species live in the southern hemisphere, mainly at the South Pole. They can also be found on the coasts of South America, the Galapagos Islands, Australia, Africa and New Zealand. In total, there might be as many as 100 million penguins in the world! Just imagine if they were all huddled together in one place!

Penguins waddle when they walk. They have black and white feathers and a torpedo-shaped body that helps them to speed through the water (they can travel at speeds of up to 25 miles an hour!). Most of the time penguins are in the water looking for food. They are excellent swimmers: they can spin, jump and dive whilst searching for food, but they cannot swim backwards! They can hold their breath underwater for about six minutes. When moving from the water to the land, they can launch themselves six feet into the air.

A penguin's main diet is fish but they also eat squid, krill and crustaceans. They have a hook at the end of their bill which helps them to grab their food. They also have bristles that face backwards on their tongues to stop slippery seafood from getting away. Penguins have a special gland in their bodies that takes the salt out of the seawater they drink, so that they actually swallow filtered water!

1 Use a dictionary or another information source to write definitions for the words in the box below. (4 marks)

> species southern hemisphere krill crustaceans

2 On which coasts can penguins be found? Choose **two** answers from the options below. (1 mark)

Africa   **Wales**   **New Zealand**   **India**

Test yourself

3 Write a sub-heading that could be used for the final paragraph. (1 mark)

4 Why does it only say there 'might' be as many as 100 million penguins in the world? (2 marks)

5 What helps penguins to 'speed through the water'? Choose **one** answer from the options below. (1 mark)

shape of their beaks   **shape of their heads**

shape of their bodies   **type of feathers**

Challenge yourself

6 What is different about the water that penguins actually swallow, compared with the water that other sea creatures drink? (1 mark)

7 Find another non-fiction book or Internet page about penguins and write **three** facts about one of the species of penguins. (2 marks)

Structure of non-fiction texts

The way in which non-fiction text is **structured** helps the reader to understand it.

Paragraphs are a great tool for structuring text, as they allow the writer to break up the text into smaller sections that focus on different ideas.

Sub-headings can also be added to the start of each paragraph to signal what the paragraph is about.

Outer Space

The Solar System is the name that we give to the Sun and everything that travels around it. This includes the eight main planets – Mercury, Venus, Earth, Mars, Jupiter, Saturn, Uranus, Neptune – and their moons. It also includes dwarf planets, such as Pluto, and their moons, as well as comets and asteroids and other objects such as satellites and rubbish from spacecraft. The path of a planet around the Sun is called its orbit. The orbits of the planets are not circles but ellipses (oval shapes).

The Sun is about 4,600,000,000 years old and has a diameter of about 1,392,500 kilometres. If you imagine the Earth is the size of a golf ball, then in comparison the Sun would be the size of a beach ball! The surface temperature of the Sun is about 5,500°C. It takes just over 8 minutes for the rays from the Sun to reach us on Earth, although we only receive a tiny fraction of the energy that the Sun gives out.

Mercury is closest to the Sun, which makes it hard for us to see it. It can reach a temperature of 350°C during the day, making it impossible for life to exist there. At night it drops to below –170°C! Whilst it takes 365.25 days (one year) for the Earth to travel around the Sun, it only takes 88 days for Mercury to travel around the Sun as it is so much closer to it.

1 Write a sub-heading that could be used for each of the three paragraphs.   (2 marks)

2 If a paragraph was needed for each of the main planets, how many more
paragraphs would be needed?   (1 mark)

Test yourself

3 What temperature can it reach on Mercury in the daytime?
Choose **one** answer from the options below.   (1 mark)

   –170°C   350°C   365.25°C   88°C

4 What shape are the orbits of the planets? Choose **one** answer from the
options below.   (1 mark)

   cuboidical   spherical   eggitical   elliptical

5 How many days would one year be on Mercury? Choose **one** answer from
the options below.   (1 mark)

   365.25   350   88   5500

6 Find **one fact** from the report about the Sun.   (1 mark)

Challenge yourself

7 What type of text is this? Choose **one** answer from the options below.
Explain your answer clearly.   (2 marks)

   recount   explanation   discussion   instructions

8 A mnemonic is a way of remembering an important piece of information.
For example, 'Naughty Elephants Squirt Water' helps you to remember the
order of points on a compass – North, East, South, West. Write a mnemonic
to remember the order of the planets in the solar system.   (1 mark)

Presentation and meaning

You can pick up a great deal from text simply by glancing at the way it is **presented**. For example, instructions to make something usually have a list of materials required, followed by numbered steps using imperative verbs (also known as 'bossy verbs' – they tell people what to do!) and, sometimes, diagrams. At a glance, the reader can identify the text as a list of instructions without having to read anything.

Frozen Fruit Sticks with Blackberry Sauce

Ingredients

For the fruit sticks:

100g strawberries, cut in half

100g mango, cut into chunks

100g melon, cut into chunks

2 kiwi fruits peeled and cut into chunks

For the blackberry sauce:

250g blackberries

50g golden caster sugar

½ teaspoon vanilla extract

Method

1. Put the blackberries and sugar into a small saucepan with 100ml water.

2. Bring to the boil, then simmer for 5 minutes until the fruit is soft.

3. Stir in the vanilla extract, remove and cool a little.

4. Put the fruit on wooden sticks.

5. Put the sticks into the freezer for 1 hour until they are just starting to freeze.

6. Whilst the fruit is in the freezer, tip the contents of the pan into a food processor and make it into a purée.

7. Strain the purée through a sieve to make it smooth.

8. Put into a jug ready to serve.

9. Take the sticks out of the freezer and serve with the sauce.

1 What type of text is this? How do you know? (1 mark)

2 Why do you think the ingredients are listed first? (1 mark)

Test yourself

3 How many grams of blackberries are needed? Choose **one** answer from the options below. (1 mark)

100 **250** **50** **200**

4 After stirring in the vanilla extract, what do you have to do? Choose **one** answer from the options below. (1 mark)

stir it **eat it** **mix it** **cool it**

5 How many different ingredients are needed to make just the fruit sticks? Choose **one** answer from the options below. (1 mark)

6 **5** **4** **3**

6 Write **one** imperative verb that is used in the text. (1 mark)

7 Would you like to make the fruit sticks? Explain your answer using the text. (2 marks)

Challenge yourself

8 Write the word that is used to show that you make the sauce at the same time as the fruit is freezing. (1 mark)

9 What will be left in the sieve when the puree has gone through it? (1 mark)

How did you do?

Structure and meaning

Non-fiction texts are **structured** based on their purpose (the reason why they are written), as well as taking into account the audience (who they are written for). For example, a newspaper report often has a headline, a picture with a caption and then a report written in columns. The first paragraph often answers the basic questions: who, what, where, when and why?

Doughnut-tastic!

It is quite common to read about children's sporting and academic achievements. However, a child achieving a world record in balancing doughnuts on his head is almost unheard of. But that is what Harry Jones from Barnstaple received an award for this week.

The award was given to the 14 year old by the Guinness World Records team when they arrived in Barnstaple to verify his unusual claims. Harry had been working at the record since the age of 10, when he became obsessed with the little, round, sugary treats! While other youngsters spent their free time at the park, watching TV, or playing on games consoles, Harry saved his pocket money to buy doughnuts to balance on his head. He soon realised that he needed a trusty companion to help him to reach his goal. This is when he gave the important role of 'doughnut support person' to his older brother.

By the age of 12 he was able to balance 12 doughnuts on his head; by the age of 13 he had doubled this to 24 doughnuts; and by the time he reached 14, when he was ready to have his record verified, he could balance an amazing 44 doughnuts on top of his head.

Speaking of his achievement, he said, 'I am happy with it for now as it has set a baseline for the record. I still want to go further, or even try balancing different things on my head.'

Watch this space for what he is going to attempt next!

Harry during his record attempt

1 What words make up the caption in this report? (1 mark)

2 Write answers to the following questions about this article. (2 marks)

Who?

What?

Where?

When?

Why?

Test yourself

3 How many doughnuts could Harry balance on his head when he was 14? Choose **one** answer from the options below. (1 mark)

14   **12**   **44**   **24**

4 What is Harry's surname? Choose **one** answer from the options below. (1 mark)

Smith   **Jones**   **Harry**   **Barnstaple**

5 Write an alternative headline for this article. (1 mark)

6 Would you like to attempt this record? Explain your answer with clear reasons, based on details in the report. (2 marks)

Challenge yourself

7 Do you think Harry had lots of friends before he broke the world record? Explain your answer. (2 marks)

8 Write a quote from Harry's brother to show how he feels about Harry's achievement that could be included in the report. (1 mark)

How did you do?

Bottle Marvel!

A bottle with a century-old message inside was found by a couple in Germany in April 2016. The bottle was washed up on a beach on the German island of Amrum.

The bottle contained a postcard asking that it be sent to the Marine Biological Association of the UK. The couple complied with the wishes of the writer.

It was tossed into the North Sea sometime between 1904 and 1906 and has been bobbing around in the vast area of water until it washed ashore 108 years later.

When asked to comment, a spokesperson for the

The well-travelled bottle

Marine Biological Association of the UK said, 'This bottle was one of 1,000 released as part of our research into ocean currents. Each bottle was weighed down so that it would float just above the seabed. It is truly astonishing that we have received this bottle 108 years after it was thrown into the ocean. We believe it to be the oldest message in a bottle ever to be found. As promised on the postcard, we have sent an old shilling to the couple who found the bottle! Most of the other bottles were returned to us many years ago by fishermen. We are waiting to hear whether this is a new world record. Fingers crossed!'

The present world record for the oldest message in a bottle is 99 years and 43 days. This bottle was found west of the Shetland Islands in July 2013.

Reporter: Matt Ingram

1. What type of non-fiction text is this? Choose **one** answer from the options below. (1 mark)

   recipe   **instructions**   **newspaper**   **leaflet**   **poster**

2. Identify **two** features of this type of text. (2 marks)

3. Identify the words of the caption. (1 mark)

4. Which words are subject-specific in this report? Choose **three** answers from the options below. (2 marks)

   seabed   **comment**   **biological**   **ocean**   **spokesperson**

5. Where was the bottle found? (1 mark)

6. Was the spokesperson for the Marine Biological Association of the UK pleased to receive the bottle? Explain your answer. (3 marks)

7. What reward did the postcard say it would give people who returned the card to the Marine Biological Association of the UK? (1 mark)

8. Find the phrase from paragraph 2 which shows that the couple sent the bottle back to where the postcard asked them to. (1 mark)

9. Who is the audience for this report? Choose **one** answer from the options below. (1 mark)

   • The Biological Association
   • The couple who found the bottle
   • The public

10. What is the purpose of this report? (1 mark)

11. Write a summary of the report in no more that **50** words. (3 marks)

Score ◯ /17   43

Acknowledgements

The author and publisher are grateful to the copyright holders for permission to use quoted materials and images.

Page 4 from *Swallows and Amazons* by Arthur Ransome, published by Jonathan Cape, reprinted by permission of The Random House Group Limited; except in the USA: reprinted by permission of David R. Godine, Publisher, Inc © 1930 by Arthur Ransome.

Page 10 'The Midas Touch' adapted with the kind permission of Joel Skidmore, Mythweb (http://www.mythweb.com).

Page 14 from *The Lion, the Witch and the Wardrobe* by C. S. Lewis, copyright © C. S. Lewis Pte. Ltd. 1950. Extract reprinted by permission.

Page 20 'The Lion and the Mouse' and page 24 'Weird is the Woman', reproduced with the kind permission of Alison Head.

Published by Keen Kite Books
An imprint of HarperCollins*Publishers* Ltd
1 London Bridge Street
London SE1 9GF

ISBN 9780008161712

First published in 2015

10 9 8 7 6 5 4 3 2 1

Text and design © 2015 Keen Kite Books, an imprint of HarperCollins*Publishers* Ltd

Author: Rachel Axten-Higgs

The author asserts his moral right to be identified as the author of this work.

All rights reserved. No part of this publication may be reproduced, stored in a retrieval system, or transmitted, in any form or by any means, electronic, mechanical, photocopying, recording or otherwise, without the prior permission of Keen Kite Books.

Series Concept and Commissioning: Michelle I'Anson
Series Editor and Development: Shelley Teasdale
Inside Concept Design: Paul Oates
Project Manager: Jane Moody
Cover Design: Carolyn Gibson
Text Design and Layout: Q2A Media
Production: Niccolò de Bianchi
Printed in Great Britain by Martins the Printers, Berwick upon Tweed

A CIP record of this book is available from the British Library.

Images are ©Shutterstock.com